fishes we know

by the Editors of Creative
A CREATIVE EDUCATION MINI BOOK

Distributed Exclusively by
CHILDRENS PRESS, CHICAGO

Photographic Credits:
Page 6, Rosenthal from Rapho Guillwmette; Page 11, Treat Davidson from National Audubon Society; Page 15, Loren P. Woods; Page 18, Harold M. Lambert Studios; Page 23, John Hugemeyer from Black Star; Page 30, Ronald L. Mrowiec.

ISBN: 0-87191-243-0
Library of Congress Catalog Card Number: 73-4537

contents

TROUT

Fishes are cold-blooded animals, with a body temperature that matches their environment. Trout prefer cooler waters, and some kinds will not thrive where the water becomes warmer than 50° F. All live in fresh water; but the rainbow, Dolly Varden, and cutthroat come downstream and enter the sea.

Like all fish, the trout breathes by taking in water through its mouth and expelling it through the gill openings. Gills have feathery membranes able to take oxygen from the passing water and give up carbon dioxide waste from the body of the fish. Cold water contains more oxygen than warm, and trout "smother" if placed in water too warm for them.

Trout feed on small living things such as insects, worms, crayfish, tadpoles, frogs, and fish smaller than themselves. As fishermen know, trout seem to have "favorite" foods during certain times of the year. The temperature, the weather, and the season all affect the appetite of the fish.

Trout are beautiful, excellent to eat, and fun to catch because they are so wary and fight so hard when hooked. They can only live in clean waters. Pollution caused by man and his cities is deadly to the trout. Before European settlers came to North America, trout where found in streams, rivers, and lakes wherever the waters were cool. Now they have disappeared from many parts of their former range. But efforts are being made to clean up the waterways and bring the trout back. Government agencies have hatcheries that raise young trout in special tanks. They are then set free in the wild. Commercial trout farms raise the fish for food and for people to catch.

The beautiful brook trout can live only in cold, unpolluted waters. It is becoming rare in places where man makes his home.

MATING AND HAVING YOUNG

Male and female trout swim to clear, cold waters to spawn, or produce young. They select a place where there is fine gravel on the bed of a stream or lake. The female pours eggs out of her body and the male, swimming nearby, pours out a substance called milt which covers the eggs and fertilizes them. Then the parent fish swim away.

Many of the eggs are eaten by enemies before they hatch. But some develop into young, called fry. Fry hatch in 30 to 45 days. At first the tiny fish has a yolk sac attached to its abdomen. It does not eat, but hides and grows for about a month. Then the yolk is all gone and the little fish must begin to seek small living things for food. Trout 2 or 3 inches long are called fingerlings. They continue to grow all their lives;

7

but very large trout are seldom caught nowadays. The average size for all except lake and Dolly Varden trout is only a pound or so.

DIFFERENT KINDS OF TROUT

North American trout are all more or less speckled. But their actual coloring varies from place to place. The brook trout is native to the East. The rainbow trout, with a pink band along the side, is native to the West. Dolly Varden trout, native to Pacific Coast streams, resemble brook trout but are larger. The most beautiful trout is the golden trout from the high Rockies. It is greenish-gold above, with red lower fins and many black spots on the tail and dorsal fin. Lake trout, from the Great Lakes, are dark green or blue with wiggly, light-colored markings.

catfish

Many fish have their skins studded with scales — horny growths that provide protection from enemies. But the sturdy catfish are clothed only in tough, leathery hide. An enemy that attempts to grasp them may be pierced or even poisoned by defensive spines growing from the catfish's fins. The barbels, growing about the mouth, are harmless sensory organs. As the fish cruises along the bottom of a river or lake, the barbels feel and smell about in the mud for bits of food.

Catfish are scavengers, helping to keep the waterways clean of dead animals. Catfish are very tough and can endure muddy or polluted water that would be fatal to more delicate species.

In some parts of the U.S., catfish are "farmed." Not particular as to the kind of food they receive, catfish may be raised in ponds or tanks and harvested for market. When they live in clean water, they have a delicious flavor and are especially favored in the South. Fishing for catfish is an important industry in some states.

Sportsmen do not consider the catfish to be a fighting fish. But many people enjoy catching them because they are easily taken on many different kinds of bait. A simple pole, line and hook baited with a worm will catch a catfish. The fish must be skinned before cooking.

RAISING YOUNG

Some kinds of catfish, including the black bullhead shown in the picture, take care of their newly hatched young. Eggs are laid by the female and then fertilized by the male. He continues to guard them, puffing fresh water over them as they develop and even taking them in his mouth from time to time to clean

them. After the fry hatch they group together in a school that may number several hundred. The father stays near them, guarding them from enemies, for many weeks. Rarely, the female will take over the job.

The males of sea catfish carry the eggs around in the mouth until the young hatch. The father does not eat during this time. He may also carry the newly hatched young in his mouth. A strange South American catfish has a different way of guarding its eggs. Each egg has a stalk, which attaches to the belly of the mother fish. She carries them until hatching.

By guarding the eggs and the young, the catfish parents insure that more young fish will survive. This is one of the reasons why catfish are so abundant all over the world.

DIFFERENT KINDS OF CATFISH

The large catfish family (Siluridae) contains both freshwater and saltwater kinds. Some of them, such as the electric catfish of Africa and the walking catfish, which can live on land for some time, are very unusual.

Among the best-known catfish are the small bullheads. The black bullhead is brownish-black or speckled, found from Hudson Bay to the Gulf of Mexico in slow-moving streams, rivers, and ponds. Brown and yellow bullheads are similar. The channel catfish prefers clean rivers on the Atlantic Coast or in the Mississippi Valley. It is gray with scattered black spots. The largest North American catfish is the blue catfish of the Mississippi and other southern rivers. It is blue-gray above and silvery below and may reach a weight of over 150 lbs.

sunfish

Fresh, shallow waters that are not too cold appeal to the little sunfish. They are among the most common inhabitants of small lakes and ponds, and will live in city lagoons and artificial farm ponds as well. Sunfish belong to the bass family (Centrarchidae). Even though they are small, they are favored by young fishermen because they are fighters, easy to catch, and good to eat.

Sunfish have a rather oval silhouette. The end of the dorsal fin is rounded and "matches" the rounded anal fin below the tail.

Sunfish feed on insects, tiny crustaceans, and other little water animals, moving in the sunny shallows either singly or in schools. They must be wary because larger fish, such as pike and bass, are waiting to snap them up for food.

14

HAVING YOUNG

Many kinds of sunfish make nests. The male pumpkinseed scrapes a saucer-shaped hole in the bottom of a pond, then lures a female to it. As she lays her eggs, he pours his milt onto them to fertilize them. Then he chases her away and finds a second female. His nest may have the eggs of three or four mothers in it at the end. Then the male guards them carefully until they hatch.

He also guards the fry, but is not as faithful a parent as the male bullhead. Before long, the infant sunfish are on their own, feeding on microscopic water creatures and dodging enemies such as birds, frogs, and larger fish.

DIFFERENT KINDS OF SUNFISH

All sunfish have a similar body shape. But their color varies greatly from place to place. Sunfish that have different colors may mate and produce young that bear some resemblance to both parents. In some parts of the country sunfish are called bream.

The bluegill sunfish usually has a gray-blue face, bluish fins and gray-blue bars along its sides. The pumpkinseed or common sunfish resembles the bluegill but has less distinct markings on its sides. The warmouth sunfish's body is gray-green with golden streaks and spots. Yellow stripes extend out from its red eyes. The green sunfish has barred sides and a gray-green color. It is very common and seldom grows to be more than 6 inches long.

17

Yellowfin tuna are important food fish in
many parts of the world.

tuna

Built for speed, the sleek tuna charges through the sea like
a torpedo, catching food animals such as herring, mackerel,
and squid. Its body is smooth and nearly scaleless. Huge old
bluefin tuna are among the largest of bony fishes. (The whale
shark, largest of all fishes, has a skeleton of flexible cartilage.)
The largest bluefin ever taken weighed about 1,600 pounds
and was 14 feet long. Bluefins commonly weigh 400 pounds.

These powerful, carnivorous fish belong to the mackerel
family (Scombridae). They are found in all warm seas of the
world and migrate, or undertake regular yearly journeys.
Younger tuna travel in schools, while the giant fish often swim
alone. Because of their size and speed, tuna have few natural
enemies. Killer whales are said to attack them sometimes.

SPAWNING

The mating and spawning habits of the tuna are still not well known. By tagging the fish, scientists have learned that they tend to keep in separate groups. The tuna of North American waters apparently spawn off the Bahama Islands, while European tuna spawn near the Azores. There is some mixing of the populations, however.

Warm tropical waters are full of plankton, tiny drifting plants and animals. Young tuna feed on tiny creatures such as shrimp and copepods, growing very quickly because of the abundant food. In May and June, the larger tuna migrate to colder waters in search of schools of fish such as sardines, herring, and menhaden. They usually stay in deep water.

TUNA FISHING

The catching of tuna is an important industry in many parts of the world. Most of the giant fish are canned. California tuna boats, called clippers, are large sea-going craft that may travel as far as South America in their search for the migrating fish. A lookout stationed in a crow's nest high above the deck watches for signs of a school. When one is sighted, the crew release bait fish — small anchovies — into the water. The tuna come swarming around the clipper and are caught with hook and line. The hooks are barbless, "baited" with a bunch of feathers. Two or more poles are often attached to a single hook so that several men can work at hauling the huge fish in. Commercial fishermen also take tuna by means of nets.

TROPICAL FISHES

Early in the 1900's, small, colorful freshwater fishes began to be common pets. Most of them were caught in South America in tropical rivers and shipped northward in tanks. With the passing of years, keeping tropical fish became a favorite hobby of many people. Hundreds of different kinds are now available to collectors. They can be purchased in pet stores and department stores everywhere.

One of the most popular kinds is the freshwater angelfish, or scalare. It is very common in the waters of the Amazon River, living in schools of a dozen or so. A male and female become a mated pair, staying together for many years.

Another popular tropical species is the platy, whose name is an abbreviation of its former scientific name. It is closely related to the swordtails, and the two kinds of fish can be cross-

bred. Platys are native to rivers in Central America. The wild platy is rather plain; but through the years, breeders have produced the colorful kinds shown in the picture — and many others besides.

The beautiful little neon tetra is native to the cool, dark waters of the Upper Amazon basin. When in shadow, it appears drab. But if light strikes its body it shows a beautiful blue stripe like a tiny neon light.

KEEPING TROPICAL FISH

Some kinds of tropical fish, such as guppies and Siamese fighting fish, can live in an ordinary bowl with plants. But most tropicals need extra oxygen in the water. They do best in an aquarium that holds at least five gallons. The water must be treated to remove the chlorine that is added by city water-treatment plants. Then the tank is given a floor of gravel, with plants, and allowed to settle for a day. An air bubbler, usually with a water filter attached, is placed in a rear corner of the tank. The temperature of the water is kept above 70 degrees, with a heater if necessary, and most fish fanciers have a thermometer in the tank. Water plants require light, and a lamp is usually mounted on top.

It is possible to keep many different kinds of tropical fish together in one tank. But when buying a new kind of fish, one should try to find out whether or not it will live peacefully with others.

Tropical fish will stay healthy if a few simple rules are followed. The tank should not be too crowded. The fishes should not be given too much food, since uneaten leftovers sink to the bottom and decay, fouling the water. Waste matter should be removed from the bottom of the tank from time to time to keep the water clean and fresh. A good water filter helps in this task, and it should be cleaned regularly.

When a new fish is purchased, it should not be added to the tank at once. Instead, it should stay by itself for a week or so to make sure that it does not have a disease. If a fish does become sick, it is often possible to treat it with medicines available in pet stores.

BREEDING TROPICAL FISH

Many kinds of tropical fish breed in captivity. Among the easiest to breed are guppies, platys, and mollies. These do not lay eggs, but rather give birth to living young. The adult fish must be kept separate from the babies or they will eat the young.

When living in the wild, baby fish can escape the adults by hiding among the plants. But this is not easy to do in a crowded tank.

Angelfish will also breed in captivity, laying eggs on plant leaves. Both parents fan water over them and take them into the mouth to clean them. When the fry hatch, the parents usually guard them — but sometimes they try to eat them.

Sometimes a species of tropical fish will refuse to breed in captivity. It may be discovered that the fish requires very special conditions of water temperature and water quality before breeding. Or it may need special plants or some other kind of special environment before producing young. Neon tetras did not breed in captivity until someone discovered that they needed soft water.

Largemouth BASS

One of the favorites of sport fishermen in North America, the largemouth bass has been introduced into fresh waters of Canada, the U.S., and Mexico. It was originally native to slow-flowing streams and ponds of Mississippi Valley, Great Lakes region, Gulf Coast, and Florida. The largest come from southern waters. Related to sunfish and crappies, bass belong to the family Centrarchidae.

The bass is a hunter, seeking smaller fish such as bluegills, as well as frogs, crayfish, ducklings, and even baby muskrats. It cruises quietly about until it sees its prey, then opens its huge mouth and gulps the victim down. Smaller bass have many enemies, and may be devoured by the very animals they prey upon when full-grown.

Largemouth bass may be grown artificially in a farm pond. The pond is fertilized to encourage the growth of plants. Tiny water creatures, called plankton, feed on the plants and on each other. Then the pond is stocked with bluegills, which feed on the smaller animals, and with bass, which feed on the bluegills. Fishermen must catch the bass if they are not to become too numerous. If it is properly maintained, a farm pond such as this becomes entirely self-sufficient, producing generation after generation of plants and animals that feed upon each other in an unbroken chain of life. But the pond cannot succeed unless the fisherman remains part of the chain. If too few bass are taken, they will multiply, eat all the bluegills, and begin to starve. If too many bass are taken, the bluegills will multiply too fast. They will eat the baby bass and eventually the pond will have only bluegills. Bass have been reared in hatcheries and introduced into warmer waters all over North America.

The mouth of the largemouth bass extends
beyond its eye. This identifies the fish.

RAISING YOUNG

A male bass coaxes a female to lay her eggs in a place he
has chosen. Then he pours milt on them to fertilize them and
chases the female away. She has nothing more to do with her
offspring. It is the father bass that guards the eggs, chasing
away any hungry fish that may come near. When the eggs
hatch, the male continues his guard duty. The babies eat insect
larvae, tiny crustaceans, and other microscopic plankton animals. Later, when they are several inches long, the young can
fend for themselves. A year-old bass is about 6 inches long.
It is twice as big and full-grown at two years of age. Bass may
live for nearly 20 years, growing all the time.

Other Creative Mini Books

Life Cycles

Life Cycle of a Bullfrog
Life Cycle of a Raccoon
Life Cycle of an Opossum
Life Cycle of a Moth
Life Cycle of a Rabbit
Life Cycle of a Fox
Life Cycle of a Turtle
Life Cycle of a Butterfly

World We Know

Fishes We Know
Birds We Know
Reptiles We Know
Mammals We Know
Insects We Know

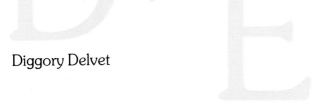

Diggory Delvet

Flopsy Bunnies

Kep

Lucie

Miss Moppet

Peter Rabbit's
A B C

With new reproductions from the original illustrations by

BEATRIX POTTER

F. WARNE & Cº

a is for apples

"Cecily Parsley brewed good cider (from apples)."

Unpublished picture for *Cecily Parsley's Nursery Rhymes*

b is for butter

"Ribby went out down the field to the farm,
to fetch some milk and butter."

From *The Tale of The Pie and The Patty-Pan*

c is for carrot

"This is a nice gentle Rabbit.
His mother has given him a carrot."

From *The Story of A Fierce Bad Rabbit*

Dd

d is for ducks

"The three Puddle-ducks came along the hard
high road, marching one behind the other."

From *The Tale of Tom Kitten*

Ee

e is for eggs

"Eggs, new-laid! Fresh new-laid eggs!"

From *The Tale of Little Pig Robinson*

f is for flowers

"'How do you do, my dear Ribby?' said Duchess.
'I've brought you some flowers.'"

From *The Tale of The Pie and The Patty-Pan*

Gg

g is for gate

Gg

"Peter, who was very naughty, ran straight away
to Mr. McGregor's garden, and squeezed under the gate!"

From *The Tale of Peter Rabbit*

h is for ham

"Tom Thumb set to work at
once to carve the ham."

From *The Tale of Two Bad Mice*

i is for ink

Ii

" Dr. Maggotty was occupied
in putting rusty nails into a bottle of ink."

From *The Tale of The Pie and The Patty-Pan*

j is for jacket

"Mr. McGregor hung up the little jacket and
the shoes for a scare-crow."

From *The Tale of Peter Rabbit*

k is for kittens

"Once upon a time, there were three little kittens,
and their names were Mittens, Tom Kitten and Moppet."

From *The Tale of Tom Kitten*

L l

l is for ladybird

"'Ladybird, ladybird, fly away home,
Your house is on fire and your children all gone'"

From *The Tale of Mrs. Tittlemouse* and *Beatrix Potter's Nursery Rhyme Book*

m is for mouse

Mm

"The mouse watches Miss Moppet
from the top of the cupboard."

From *The Story of Miss Moppet*

Nn

n is for newspaper

"Seated upon a stump, she was startled to find
an elegantly-dressed gentleman, reading a newspaper."

From *The Tale of Jemima Puddle-Duck*

Oo

o is for oranges

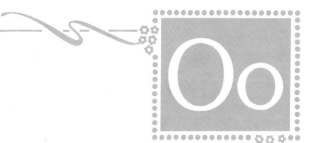

"There were two red lobsters and a ham, a fish,
a pudding, and some pears and oranges."

From *The Tale of Two Bad Mice*

P p

p is for pigs

"And the other two little boy pigs,
Pigling Bland and Alexander, went to market."

From *The Tale of Pigling Bland*

q is for quilt

"Hunca Munca has got the cradle (and a quilt)
and some of Lucinda's clothes."

From *The Tale of Two Bad Mice*

Rr

r is for rabbits

Rr

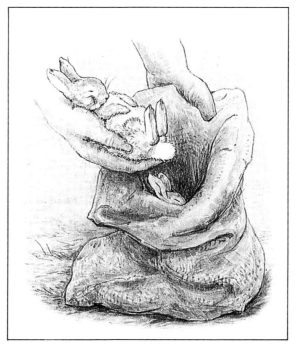

"'One, two, three, four! five! six leetle rabbits!'
said he as he dropped them into his sack."

From *The Tale of The Flopsy Bunnies*

Ss

s is for strawberry

Ss

"Timmy Willie had been reared on roots and salad
(and sometimes a strawberry)."

From *The Tale of Johnny Town-Mouse*

t is for tea-cup

"Out from under tea-cups and from under bowls and
basins, stepped other and more little mice."

From *The Tailor of Gloucester*

Illustration by Beatrix Potter for *A Happy Pair,* by F. Weatherley

u is for umbrella

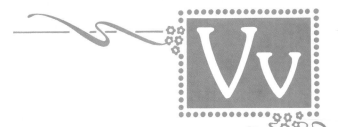

From *The Tale of Johnny Town-Mouse*

v is for violets

From *The Tale of Mrs. Tiggy-Winkle*

w is for washing

From *The Tale of Jemima Puddle-Duck*

x is in fox

Yy

From *The Tale of Mrs. Tiggy-Winkle*

y is for yard

From *The Tale of Mrs. Tittlemouse*

z is for "Zzz, bizz!"

FREDERICK WARNE

Published by the Penguin Group
27 Wrights Lane, London W8 5TZ, England
Penguin Books USA Inc., 375 Hudson Street, New York, New York 10014, USA
Penguin Books Australia Ltd, Ringwood, Victoria, Australia
Penguin Books Canada Ltd, 10 Alcorn Avenue, Toronto, Ontario, Canada M4V 3B2
Penguin Books (N.Z.) Ltd, 182-190 Wairau Road, Auckland 10, New Zealand

Penguin Books Ltd, Registered Offices: Harmondsworth, Middlesex, England

First published by Frederick Warne & Co. 1987
Reissued 1998
1 3 5 7 9 10 8 6 4 2

Endpapers designed and produced by Colin Twinn
Additional artwork (details) by Colin Twinn

ISBN 0 7232 3423 X

Printed and bound in Singapore

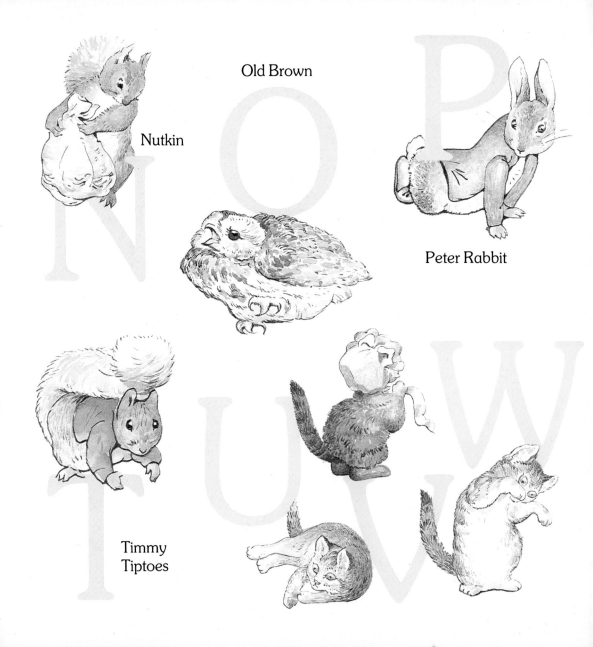

Nutkin

Old Brown

Peter Rabbit

Timmy
Tiptoes